ESSENTIAL 101 TIPS

BABY
CARE

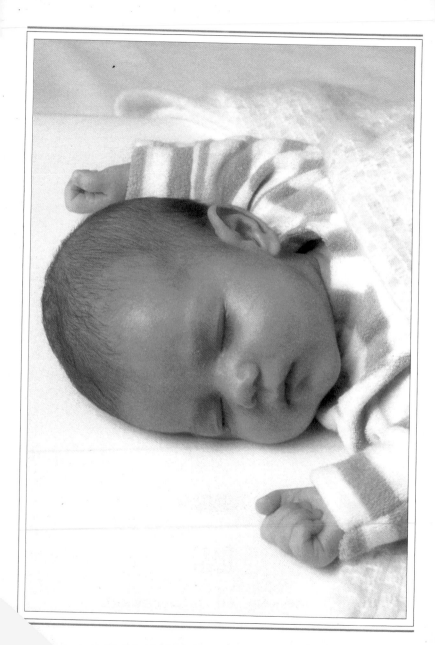

ESSENTIAL **101** TIPS

BABY CARE

Elizabeth Fenwick

DORLING KINDERSLEY

London • New York • Sydney • Moscow

A DORLING KINDERSLEY BOOK

WWW.DK.COM

Editor James Harrison
Art Editor Sharon Rudd
Series Editor Charlotte Davies
Series Art Editor Clive Hayball
Production Controller Lauren Britton

First published in Great Britain in 1996 by
Dorling Kindersley Limited,
9 Henrietta Street, London WC2E 8PS

4 6 8 10 9 7 5

A CIP catalogue record for this book is available from the British Library.

ISBN 0-7513-0278-3

Text film output by The Right Type, Great Britain
Reproduced by Colourscan, Singapore
Printed and bound by Graphicom, Italy

ESSENTIAL TIPS

HANDLING YOUR NEW BABY

1 PICKING UP A NEWBORN

To calm and reassure your baby, as well as yourself, make eye contact and talk soothingly to her before you pick her up. If you snatch your baby suddenly, you will startle her. Slide one hand underneath her to support her lower back and bottom. From the opposite side, slide your other hand under to support her neck and head. Take the weight of her head and body, and gently lift her into a cradling position.

THE NEED FOR YOUR SUPPORT ▷
Until your baby is about eight weeks old, she cannot control her head or muscles, so you must take the weight of her head and body.

PROTECT HER HEAD FROM FLOPPING
From a cradling position (see p.9) make sure you have one hand, with the palm open, taking the weight of her head.

2 PUTTING YOUR BABY DOWN SAFELY

Put your baby down using your whole arm to support her spine, neck, and head. Once the mat is taking her weight, you can slide your nearest hand gently from under her bottom. Use this hand to help lift her head a little so you can slide out the hand still supporting her head, and lower her head down gently on to the mat.

3 CRADLING A BABY THE NATURAL WAY

From the picking-up position, carefully transfer your baby's head to the crook of your slightly inclined arm (whichever you are comfortable with) or your shoulder.

Your wrist and hand encircle her back while your other arm lends extra support to her bottom and legs. Cradling this way means your baby can look and listen to you.

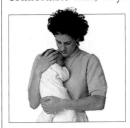

SHOULDER/BOTTOM HOLD
Hold her head to your shoulder, with one hand supporting her bottom.

CLASSIC CRADLE HOLD
Rest her head in the crook of your elbow; the other arm supports the rest of her.

BABY FACE DOWN
A baby may like being held with her chin and cheek resting on your forearm.

4 SHOULDER HUGGING

When a baby can support her head she will enjoy this close hug, with her head nestling by your head. Her arms cling on to your clothes or your neck, while you support her bottom and legs with both arms.

CALMING HUG
This is an ideal soothing hold after play; it is also good for burping a baby.

5 HOLD FROM THE HIP

By the time she is about three months old your baby can cling onto you while sitting astride your hip. This is a great hold when you are moving around, getting her milk or clothes ready. She feels close and safe, and has a good view.

SELF SUPPORTING
Your baby's knees grip your hips while your arm supports her back and bottom. This also gives you the use of a free hand.

6 GIVING GENTLE SWINGS & BOUNCES

Once your baby can lift his head and has muscle control, at around four months, you can introduce some physical play, such as swinging him above your head, perching him high on your shoulder, or bouncing him up on your knee. Just how boisterous you are depends on his temperament and mood. Be responsive to this.

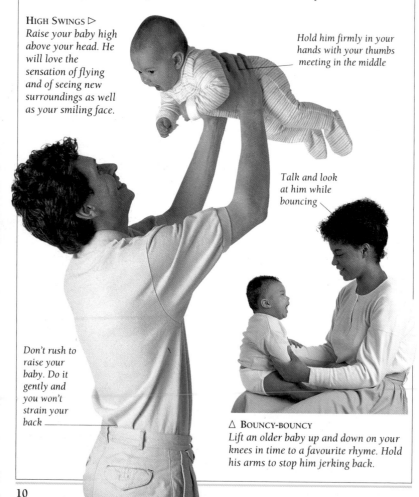

HIGH SWINGS ▷
Raise your baby high above your head. He will love the sensation of flying and of seeing new surroundings as well as your smiling face.

Hold him firmly in your hands with your thumbs meeting in the middle

Talk and look at him while bouncing

Don't rush to raise your baby. Do it gently and you won't strain your back

△ **BOUNCY-BOUNCY**
Lift an older baby up and down on your knees in time to a favourite rhyme. Hold his arms to stop him jerking back.

7 USING BOUNCERS, ROCKERS & WALKERS

Baby bouncers and walkers are useful for supervised play. They give baby sensations of movement while giving your arms a much needed rest. Baby walkers should not be used unsupervised, or on slippery or raised surfaces. Once your baby can crawl, use only for brief periods: he needs to explore freely!

Adjustable foam padded seat

◁ BABY WALKERS
Circular baby walkers are suitable for a baby who can crawl, but not for an accomplished walker. Ensure baby has a free passageway, away from any indoor hazards.

Clamps on doorway

BOUNCING CRADLES ▽
From around six weeks, let your baby spend some wakeful times in a bouncing cradle or cradle rocker on the floor. Some have attach-on head supports and clip-on toys.

Safety harness

Toes should only just touch the floor

BABY BOUNCER △
This useful playtime aid is suitable for babies from about 5 to 11 months, up to a weight of 13 kg (28 lb). A steel clamp attachment fits it on to a doorway.

11

8 HOLDING A BABY IN A SLING

For the first three months, a sling is an excellent way of carrying your baby around both indoors and outside. The close contact to your body and the motion as you walk soothes her, and it leaves your arms free.

Padded headrest is essential

Choose a padded and machine-washable sling

Let your hands reassure your baby

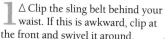

1 △ Clip the sling belt behind your waist. If this is awkward, clip at the front and swivel it around.

2 △ Sit down with her snug on your shoulder. Keep a hand behind her and put her legs in the gap.

3 △ Pull the straps up over your shoulders. Keep a hand supporting her buttocks and back.

4 △ Sit forward, support the back of her head, and slowly let the sling take her body weight.

WELCOME TO NAPPIES

9 CLEANING ESSENTIALS

Changing a nappy is not as daunting as it may seem, but you really need to have everything ready and all within reach before you start. You must have either a changing mat or folded towel placed on the floor of a warm room (if using a changing table or bed, make sure she cannot fall off). Dispose of soiled nappies, nappy liners, cotton wool, and wipes in nappy sacks; use these also to carry soiled terry nappies. Make sure you have baby wipes, or cotton wool broken off in pieces with a bowl of warm water, plus zinc and castor oil barrier cream or petroleum jelly, and a new, clean nappy.

△ CHANGING MAT
Choose a padded, plastic-covered mat for easy cleaning, with ridges to contain any spillage.

△ COTTON WOOL

△ BOWL OF WATER   △ BABY WIPES

△ BABY LOTION

△ BABY BATH LIQUID

△ BARRIER CREAM

10 WHAT ARE DISPOSABLE NAPPIES?

Disposable nappies are nappy, liner, and plastic pants all in one: they allow moisture to soak through a top layer sheet into an absorbent filling, which is protected on the outside by a waterproof backing. Key features include elasticated legs for a snug fit, and refastenable tapes so that you can check if the nappy needs changing. Buy the correct size for your baby's weight; these are clearly shown on the packaging. They are more expensive than towelling nappies but are quick and easy to put on and remove – and you save on washing and drying costs. You will be changing around ten nappies a day at first, so buy at least 70 per week.

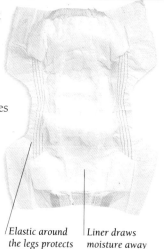

Elastic around the legs protects against leaks

Liner draws moisture away from baby's skin

11 DIFFERENT DISPOSABLES

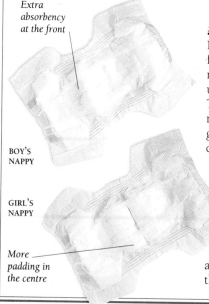

Extra absorbency at the front

BOY'S NAPPY

GIRL'S NAPPY

More padding in the centre

Nappies come in different sizes to fit a growing baby. They range from newborn 4–5 kg (up to 10 lb), right up to "junior" size at 25 kg (55 lb). There are nappies for boys with more padding at the front, and for girls, with more padding at the centre, and unisex varieties, with different absorbencies for day and night use. Choose ones with plastic waist barriers which help prevent moisture passing from the waist onto baby's clothing. "Ultra" nappies are slim, have more absorbency, but are more expensive than the bulkier standard nappies.

12 WHAT ARE TOWELLING NAPPIES?

Towelling nappies come in muslin or towelling (terry) material. You will need at least 24 of them, and you should buy the most expensive you can afford as these will be more absorbent than cheaper varieties. You must buy one-way liners to help keep baby dry, and plastic pants to prevent leaks. These are a one-off cost, but remember to account for washing and sterilizing costs after every use.

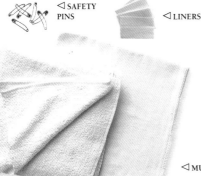

◁ SAFETY PINS

◁ LINERS

◁ MUSLIN

△ TOWEL

Natural fibre inner lining for absorbency

Plastic outer lining to prevent leaks

△ TERRY & MUSLIN NAPPIES
Terry nappies are bulkier when on than disposables, so it is advisable to buy clothes one size larger to make sure they fit. Muslin is very soft and is ideal for newborn babies.

RE-USABLE NAPPIES △
These pants fit like disposables, with re-sealable tape and elasticated legs, but they wash and wear like towelling nappies. Most have a waterproof backing so plastic pants are not needed.

△ TIE-ON PANTS
These tuck over the nappy around the waist and legs. They let air in but also leak.

△ POPPER PANTS
Once over the terry nappy, leave the bottom snaps undone so air circulates.

△ PULL-ON PANTS
These re-usable plastic pants do prevent leaks, but can encourage nappy rash.

13 CHECKING THE NAPPY CONTENTS

Babies on milk-only diets produce very loose faeces.
- For breast-fed babies, mustardy-yellow, creamy stools are normal.
- With bottle-fed babies, look for pale brown, more formed and smelly stools.
- Greenish, curd-like stools are also normal for a pre-solid-fed baby.
- Consult a doctor if the stools are very watery, or contain blood.

14 PREVENTING NAPPY RASH

Any sign of redness (with or without spots) around the bottom area is called nappy rash. The main cause is a baby being left in a wet or soiled nappy too long. So regular checking and changing is the best prevention. Make sure you clean all the skin creases and dry completely. Allow the area to "air" without a nappy for a few minutes. Wash and rinse fabric nappies thoroughly.

15 DEALING WITH NAPPY RASH

Don't feel guilty or alarmed if your baby gets nappy rash – it's very common. At the first sign of redness change nappies more frequently. With each change of nappy use a medicated baby wipe or damp cotton wool, or wool with lotion, and apply a protective cream such as zinc and castor oil ointment. If using fabric nappies, try more absorbent liners and avoid plastic pants.

Make sure all skin creases are clean and dry before applying barrier cream

Nappy rash symptoms	Likely causes	What to do
- Redness, sore-looking skin; broken skin in leg folds; smell of ammonia	- Not allowing the skin to dry well enough	- For all forms of nappy rash, start with careful drying. Don't use plastic pants. Allow time for a baby to air its genital area and bottom. Don't use powder, but use barrier cream. If this doesn't work see a doctor.
- Rash starting around the genitals rather than anus	- Urine breaking down into ammonia	
- Spotty rash all over genitals, bottom and groin	- More severe form of ammonia rash	
- Small blisters all over the nappy area	- Heat rash from sweat in skin creases	

16 CHANGING A DISPOSABLE NAPPY

Have everything ready before you start: the changing mat, a clean nappy, cotton wool and warm water or lotion or baby wipes, disposable or carrier bag for dirty nappy, barrier cream, and fresh clothes if needed. Try to make nappy changing a fun routine. It's the perfect time for some one-to-one contact, tickles, nursery games and songs. Allow time for the cleaned nappy area to dry off naturally.

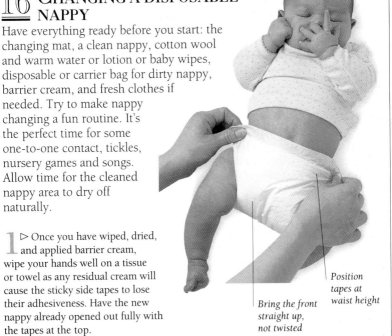

1 ▷ Once you have wiped, dried, and applied barrier cream, wipe your hands well on a tissue or towel as any residual cream will cause the sticky side tapes to lose their adhesiveness. Have the new nappy already opened out fully with the tapes at the top.

Bring the front straight up, not twisted

Position tapes at waist height

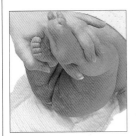

2 △ Lift the baby single-handedly by her ankles, with one finger between them. Slide the nappy top up to her waist.

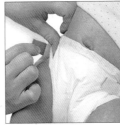

3 △ Hold one corner in position. Unpeel the tape with the other hand and pull it forwards and across the front edge.

4 △ Repeat for the other side. Modern sticky tapes allow you to unpeel and readjust to get a snug, comfortable fit.

17 CLEANING A GIRL

First wash your hands and put your baby girl on the changing mat. Undo her clothing and open out the nappy. Wipe off the worst of the faeces with a baby wipe or damp cotton wool; with a fabric nappy use a clean corner to wipe off most of the faeces. Always wipe *away* from the vaginal area towards her bottom, not the other way round. Do not try to clean inside the vaginal inner lips.

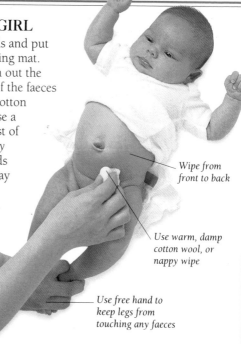

Wipe from front to back

Use warm, damp cotton wool, or nappy wipe

Use free hand to keep legs from touching any faeces

1 ▷ Lie your baby flat, open the nappy tabs and lift her legs using one hand (finger in-between her ankles). Immediately wipe the most obvious soiling on her body and then slide the nappy towards you from under her.

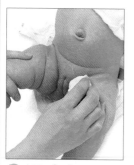

2 △ Use fresh cotton wool or wipe to clean inside all the skin creases at the top of her legs. Wipe down towards her bottom.

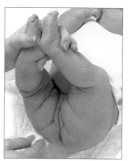

3 △ Clean her buttocks and thighs with more cotton wool, working inwards towards the anus. Keep clear of her vagina.

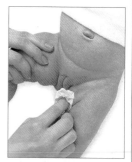

4 △ Use fingertips to dry the skin creases with wipes. Keep a soiled nappy open for dirty tissues. Fold up and seal the tapes.

18 CLEANING A BOY

The same principle of wiping from the front down towards the anus (to prevent germs reaching the genitals) also applies for boys. One big difference is not to forget the small skin areas underneath the penis and below the testicles, which often harbour traces of urine or faeces. Also, it is quite common for baby boys to urinate just as you remove the front of the nappy, so pause with the nappy held over the penis for a few seconds. Then open out the nappy and wipe any surface faeces with wipes or cotton wool, and drop them into the nappy. Then fold the soiled nappy down under him.

1 ▽ Moisten cotton wool with water or lotion and begin by wiping his tummy across, starting at the navel. Using fresh cotton wool, or a wipe, clean the creases at the top of his legs working down towards his anus and back.

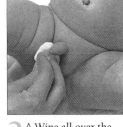

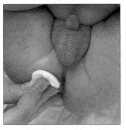

2 △ Wipe all over the testicles holding the penis out of the way. Clean under his penis.

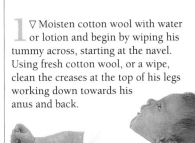

Wipe the creases from front to back

Fold the soiled nappy under him

3 △ Lift his legs by the ankles and wipe away from his anus, to buttocks and to back of thighs.

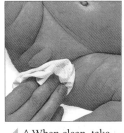

4 △ When clean, take away nappy. Dry and let him kick about and air. Apply barrier cream.

19 PREPARING FOR POTTY TRAINING

You do not have to teach a baby bowel or bladder control. It is all part of his natural development. All you have to do is encourage him and give him the opportunity to learn when he is ready. At some time in his second year your child will start to recognise the symptoms of a full rectum and a full bladder. The next step is knowing that a movement is on the way and once your child grasps this, he will quickly train himself to use the potty in time.

- Pick a time to learn when your child's life is free of new situations.
- Have a potty near by at all times.
- Praise him when he uses the potty succesfully.
- If he has an accident, don't scold.

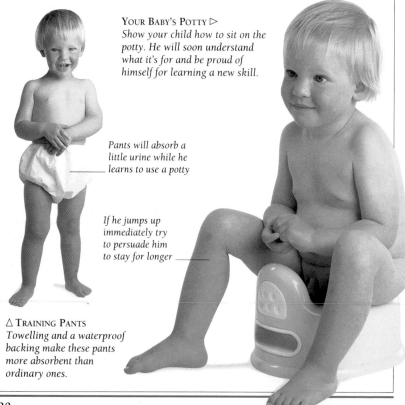

YOUR BABY'S POTTY ▷
Show your child how to sit on the potty. He will soon understand what it's for and be proud of himself for learning a new skill.

Pants will absorb a little urine while he learns to use a potty

If he jumps up immediately try to persuade him to stay for longer

△ **TRAINING PANTS**
Towelling and a waterproof backing make these pants more absorbent than ordinary ones.

20 Constipation

As your baby starts to eat a more varied diet, his stools will alter in colour and consistency. Some foods can alter the colour dramatically, but this does not mean that they are harming the baby. Your child will develop his own pattern of bowel movements. He may have a movement once or twice a day, or only once every two days. Whatever the pattern, do not try to alter it. Often parents think their child is constipated when he is not. A constipated child will pass stools less often and they will be hard enough to cause obvious discomfort when passed.

Good Sources of Fibre ▽ ▷
If your child is constipated, try to include more fibre-rich foods in his diet. This will provide the bulk that helps the bowel to grip and move its contents along.

△ Fresh Fruit
Offer your child a variety of fruits, such as slices of peeled pear, peach, and banana. They make good snacks in between meals.

△ Fresh & Lightly Cooked Vegetables
Wash vegetables well before serving. Mashed potato and broccoli are high in fibre. Celery and carrots can be given raw.

△ Dried Fruits
Prunes, apricots and other dried fruits are ideal fibre-rich treats for young children who will enjoy chewing on them.

△ Wholemeal Bread & Cereal
Choose wholemeal rather than white bread and always purée or mash cereal for a baby under eight months.

21 DIARRHOEA

Diarrhoea is the passage of very watery stools several times a day. They may look greenish and smell different from your baby's normal stools. Diarrhoea can be a serious problem for young babies because it can make them lose too much body fluid. There are a number of possible causes for mild diarrhoea but if the bowel movements return to normal after a day or two and your baby seems well and happy then there is no cause for concern.

RE-HYDRATION ▷
Make sure that your child has plenty to drink to replace lost liquid. A glucose drink is ideal.

22 WHEN TO CALL THE DOCTOR

If your baby has diarrhoea and no other symptoms, you should contact your doctor if the diarrhoea continues for more than six hours. If your baby is over a year and seems well apart from the diarrhoea you should consult your doctor if the diarrhoea shows no sign of improvement after 36 hours. If, as well as having diarrhoea, your baby is off his food, or is vomiting he may have gastroenteris, a digestive tract infection that can lead to dehydration. Call your doctor if:
- Your child has a fever and/ or is vomiting.
- Has blood in his stools.
- Seems lethargic or unwell.
- Shows any signs of dehydration, such as dry mouth and lips, the passage of small quantities of dark urine, not passing urine for six hours, sunken eyes, sunken fontanelle, abnormal drowsiness.

BATHING YOUR BABY

23 WHAT YOU NEED FOR BATHING

The most important piece of equipment is the baby bath: it must be sturdy and stable. If using a normal bath, get a rubber mat to stop baby slipping. Use only baby toiletries: these are designed to be extra mild, gently moisturizing, and have very low irritancy for delicate skins. Do not try to economize by buying adult shampoos, soaps, lotions, and creams. These have far too many additives and chemicals.

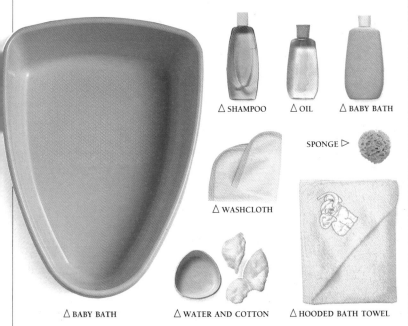

△ SHAMPOO

△ OIL

△ BABY BATH

SPONGE ▷

△ WASHCLOTH

△ BABY BATH

△ WATER AND COTTON

△ HOODED BATH TOWEL

26 HAIR WASHING WITHOUT TEARS

You should wash your newborn baby's hair every day. A clean scalp and hair will help prevent cradle cap (*see p.65*). You will need hypo-allergenic, non-sting baby shampoo, or newborn shampoo wipes (or extra mild bath lotion), a sponge, and flannel. You can also buy a specially designed plastic "halo" that fits around the hairline and prevents suds running down the face while rinsing.

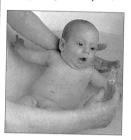

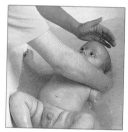

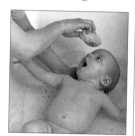

1 Use one hand to hold his head above water. Wet his hair with gentle splashes. Slide the support hand forwards and put shampoo on your palm.

2 Swap the hand supporting his head and rub shampoo until lather forms, or gently splash on lotion. Wait about 15 seconds.

3 Swap hands again and rinse off the shampoo with a damp sponge or facecloth. Wipe up and over his head away from his eyes.

27 BATH-TIME SAFETY

The most important safety feature is you: never leave your baby alone in the bath and always hold on to a very small or young child.

- Place a non-slip mat in the bottom of the bath to prevent nasty slips and slides.
- Always check the water temperature first by putting in your elbow or inner side of your wrist.
- Turn off the taps tightly. Even droplets can be scalding. Cover the hot tap with a cool flannel.
- Never top up with hot water while baby is in the bath. You can add warm water with a mixer tap.
- Do not bathe your baby in a cold room.
- Do not set the water heater thermostat too high.

△ TEMPERATURE TESTER
Use an indicator strip like this to check for an ideal 36–38°C (97–100°F).

28 GIVING A SPONGE BATH

Many babies hate having a bath or having their hair washed. If this is the case with your baby you can avoid using a bath by sponge bathing him on your lap. Start by "topping and tailing", that is, dabbing his face with fresh, moist cotton wool. Use cool, pre-boiled water for his face and warm tap water for the other parts. (*For nappy area cleaning see pp.17–19.*) Before sitting him on your lap have everything within reach.

Wear an apron to protect your clothes

Hold your baby firmly at all times

△ **TOP HALF SPONGE**
Take off his top clothes. Wet and squeeze a sponge and wash his neck. Dry it well. Wet and squeeze the sponge again for his chest and tummy.

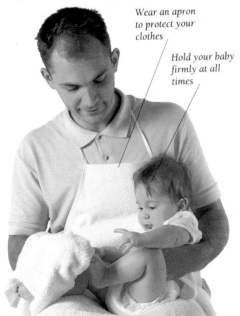

Hold arms up to flatten out skin creases

△ **LOWER HALF SPONGE**
Place a towel on your lap before you start for easy drying. Put on a clean vest for his washed top half, and take off his trousers and socks. Wash his feet, toes, and legs, and dry off thoroughly with a towel.

△ **UNDERARM WASH**
Hold his arms up to wash his underarms where sweat and fluff gather. Wash and dry his forearms also.

29 TRIMMING BABY'S FIRST NAILS

For the first few weeks the nails are so soft that you can bite them off gently yourself. Or you can try baby nail clippers or scissors. Use whichever technique makes you less nervous. With an older baby, sit him facing forwards. Hold one finger at a time and cut the nails with the scissors or clippers, following the shape of the finger-tip. For toes, cut the nail straight across.

SCISSORS WITH ROUNDED ENDS

30 FIRST TEETH & GUM CARE

Once your baby has two or more teeth, wipe them and the gums every evening with a damp handkerchief. Introduce a baby-sized toothbrush at 12 months. Clean his teeth for him after breakfast and teatime. But let him play with his toothbrush at bath-time. This should take care of the first teeth (also called "milk" teeth). Add fun and games to brushing teeth, especially by brushing your own teeth too. This will encourage your baby into the habit over time.

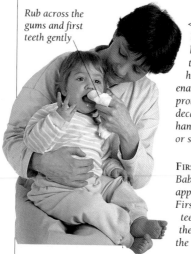

Rub across the gums and first teeth gently

◁ FIRST CLEAN
Use a pea-sized helping of fluoride toothpaste (which hardens the enamel and protects against decay) on a handkerchief or soft cloth.

FIRST TEETH ▷
Baby teeth usually appear in this order. First, or "Milk", teeth appear from the first year into the third year.

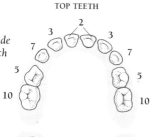

TOP TEETH

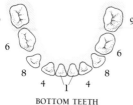

BOTTOM TEETH

DRESSING & UNDRESSING

31 ESSENTIAL HOME CLOTHING

For the first six months the all-in-one stretchsuit, sleepsuit, or romper suit will be indispensable. Make sure stretch towelling clothes are machine-washable and are made of natural fibres to help regulate body temperature. Have at least six outfits, including vests for underneath – one on, one in the wash, one spare, and three more.

VEST ▷

▽ STRETCHSUIT

△ ROMPER SUIT

△ CARDIGAN

△ SOCKS   SUN HAT△

32 CLOTHING SIZES

This is an average clothes' sizing guide.

Age	Height (up to)	Weight (up to)
New baby	55 cm (22 in)	4–5 kg (10 lb)
0–3 mths	62 cm (24 in)	6.5 kg (14 lb)
3–6 mths	68 cm (27 in)	9 kg (17.5 lb)
6–12 mths	76 cm (30 in)	11 kg (22 lb)
12–18 mths	85 cm (34 in)	12.5 kg (25 lb)

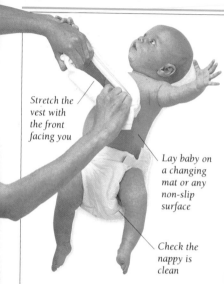

Stretch the vest with the front facing you

Lay baby on a changing mat or any non-slip surface

Check the nappy is clean

33 PUT ON A VEST

Dress him in a vest in a warm room, away from draughts. A baby feeling the air against his skin is likely to cry; do not get flustered by this. Try to make this a fun time, and use eye contact and caresses to soothe him. Dressing will get easier so try to be patient and gentle.

1 △ Lay baby on a flat, non-slip surface. Gather the vest into your hands and pull the neck apart with your thumbs. Put the back edge to his crown.

2 △ Pull the vest over his head, raising it slightly, and bring it down to his chin. Widen the arm-holes and gently guide each hand through it. Pull down.

34 TAKE OFF A VEST

After lying him down, reach through the armhole, or sleeve, to hold one elbow inside the vest with one hand. Ease all the fabric over his fist. Do the same with the other elbow. Then gather up all the vest in your hands, so there is no spare fabric that might scrape over his face. Stretch the opening as wide as you can and take it up and over his face to his crown. Now slide your hands underneath his head and neck and lift his upper body to slide out the vest.

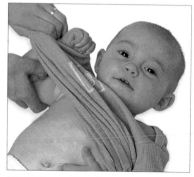

UNDRESS ON A FLAT SURFACE
Even if your baby can control his muscles and support his head, it is much easier to undress him on a mat than on your lap.

35 PUTTING ON A STRETCHSUIT

Have all poppers undone. Pick your baby up and lay the clean stretchsuit out flat underneath him. Put him back on top of the laid-out garment. Insert his legs first, then his arms. His neck should lie just above the collar.

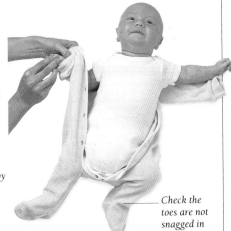

Garment laid out under baby in bodysuit

Check the toes are not snagged in the garment

1 ◁ Gather up each leg fabric and ease one foot in at a time. Place his toes right up to the end, and pull the leggings up to his crotch.

2 △ Stretch each sleeve cuff widely, then gather up and guide each fist through. Pull up the garment over his shoulders and do up the poppers.

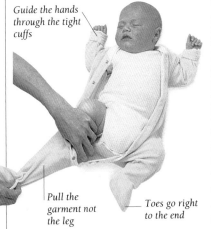

Guide the hands through the tight cuffs

Pull the garment not the leg

Toes go right to the end

36 TAKING OFF A STRETCHSUIT

Undo the poppers first and, as you bend his leg, pull the garment away from his toes. As his leg comes out, be careful not to snag his toes. Repeat with the other leg. Put your hand inside his sleeve and hold his elbow. Grasp the cuff and pull the sleeve off, keeping his arm bent. Be careful not to catch his fingers when trying to pull his hand through the cuff. Repeat with the other arm. Slide your hand under his head and neck and remove the suit.

BREAST FEEDING

37 GETTING COMFORTABLE

Breastfeeding is absolutely natural, but it still has to be learned. Much will depend on "reading" the signals your baby gives you. But you can make things far easier by getting settled for a breastfeeding session – which could last for an hour. Lying down is ideal for night-time feeds. For other sessions, seek good back support, such as sitting on a low chair with no arms, or lying up against a bed headstead with plenty of pillows behind you.

CROSS-LEGGED POSITION

38 GUIDING YOUR BABY TO LATCH ON

Once settled, take a deep breath and relax your shoulders. If in private, take off your top to make it easier for baby to "latch on", that is to be correctly placed on your breast and sucking efficiently. Use your baby's natural reflex to "root" (seek out) and to suck. If you or baby get in a muddle, soothe your baby, take another deep breath and start again.

TRIGGERING THE ROOTING REFLEX
Stroke the cheek or corner of the mouth with a finger or nipple. This will alert your baby's "rooting" reflex to find food.

FINDING THE NIPPLE
Guide your breast towards baby's tongue. To "milk" your breast, the whole of the nipple and areola should be in his mouth.

39 MANAGING YOUR MILK FLOW

Your baby doesn't just suck, she "milks" the breast by pressing on your milk supply at the base of the areola (the coloured area around the nipple). Don't worry about "supply". Your baby's sucking stimulates "demand". However, when your milk comes in, your breasts may become engorged and sore for a few days. This makes the nipple go flat so it is hard for baby to latch on. Try these steps to help baby latch on and quickly relieve any engorgement.

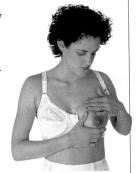

2 △ Massage the breasts and try to express some milk to relieve them if they get over-full.

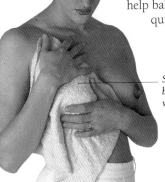

Soften your breast with a warm flannel

1 △ Lay a warm flannel or warm damp towel over each breast for several minutes. You could also take a warm bath or shower to help ease the flow.

3 △ Use your free hand on your rib cage to push upwards and make the nipple protrude so that she can get the areola in her mouth.

40 CHANGING OVER DURING A FEED

Let your baby suck for at least 10 to 15 minutes on one breast at each feed. After you've burped her, or she has had a short nap, slip a finger between her jaws to break her suction and offer her the other breast. She may be hungry enough to drain this one, too, or she may just suck for comfort. In either case, let her suck till she falls fast asleep.

41 COPING WITH LEAKING BREASTS

Your breasts may leak a lot between feeds in the early weeks. You cannot prevent this, but it will diminish as your breasts settle down and supply matches your baby's demand. To cope with this problem – and protect your clothes – wear disposable or fabric-washable breast pads inside your bra. These will absorb some of the dripping. Change the pads frequently, as wetness near your skin may make you sore.

Pads help keep your nipples dry and clean

DISPOSABLE BREAST PADS ▷
Buy shaped breast pads and be sure to wear nursing bras with wide support straps and front zip openings for easy access.

42 SOOTHING SORE NIPPLES

Sore, red nipples usually result from your baby not latching on properly. Check that she takes the whole nipple and areola area into her mouth, and that her temples and ears are moving (that is, her jaw muscles are working hard). Cracked nipples give you shooting pains during feeding, but don't stop feeds, as you may become engorged and make the problem worse.

Apply calendula cream on the area

◁ HELPFUL TREATMENTS
Use cream or antiseptic spray to relieve soreness. A plastic breast shell over your nipple inside your bra can keep the breast dry. Allow the nipple to air as much as possible also.

43 EXPRESSING MILK BY PUMP

Expressing with a purpose-made pump can work far quicker and be less tiring than hand expressing. Choose a "syringe"-type pump where the outer cylinder converts into a bottle. First soften your breasts with warm water and massage them as if expressing by hand. The feeling on your milk ducts should be like your baby's jaws.

Funnel to fit over areola and nipple

Inner cylinder

Outer cylinder

WORKING A BREAST PUMP ▷
Place the funnel of the pump over the areola to form an airtight seal. Pull the outer cylinder away from you: the suction draws milk from your breast.

MANUAL PUMP ▷

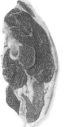

44 FOOD FOR BREAST-FEEDING MOTHERS

You will produce enough milk for your baby if you eat regularly, whenever you are hungry, drink whenever you are thirsty, and try not to become too tired. You will definitely find that you are hungrier than usual while breastfeeding – you may need as much as 800 extra calories a day. Never attempt to diet while you are breastfeeding.

MEAT △   CHEESE △

NUTS △

△ FRUIT   LIQUID △   △ FISH

45 FIRST-YEAR FEEDING ROUTINES

How long should a feed last? How many feeds should I give my baby in 24 hours? Can I tell when she is going to be hungry? Such questions are all part of the emotional and practical worries of feeding a baby in the first year. Bear in mind the following tips when planning a feeding routine:

- Always feed your baby as often as she seems hungry, and give her as much as she wants.
- For the first month at least, do not try to establish an inflexible routine.
- If you started off in the first two weeks by feeding your newborn 10 times in 24 hours (see chart), this should be reduced to eight feeds, then six, after a further six weeks.
- By two months expect to be feeding about every four hours.

- By three months plan for five feeds a day plus two night feeds.
- By four to five months plan for four feeds a day plus some solids.
- By six months your routine should be two breast-feeds a day: early morning and bedtime.
- From six months onwards your baby may be ready to be weaned off the breast (see p.48).
- By nine months you should be beginning a bedtime feed only.
- If you both want to, you can continue to breast-feed well into your baby's second year.
- Breast-fed babies usually demand more feeds than bottle-fed babies as breast milk is more easily digested than formula milk.
- If you are bottle feeding, you should be able to establish a four-hourly timetable by three months.

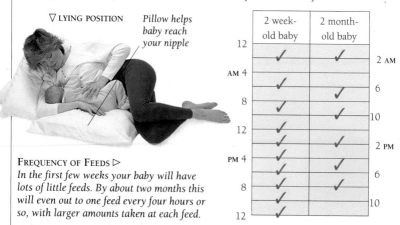

▽ LYING POSITION
Pillow helps baby reach your nipple

FREQUENCY OF FEEDS ▷
In the first few weeks your baby will have lots of little feeds. By about two months this will even out to one feed every four hours or so, with larger amounts taken at each feed.

	2 week-old baby	2 month-old baby	
12	✓	✓	2 AM
AM 4	✓		6
8	✓	✓	10
12	✓	✓	2 PM
PM 4	✓	✓	6
8	✓	✓	10
12	✓		

BOTTLE FEEDING

46 WHAT YOU NEED TO BOTTLE FEED

To ensure that bottle-feeding is a happy experience for you and your baby, you must be scrupulous about hygiene, and have everything you need – the formula milk, equipment, bibs, brushes, cleaners, and sterilizers – ready in advance. Make sure you have enough bottles, teats, and caps to make up feeds for a 24-hour period. To save time prepare all the feeds for 24 hours in one batch and store them in a refrigerator. Make up fresh feeds when you are down to two bottles of made-up feed in the refrigerator.

125 ML (4 OZ)   **250 ML (8 OZ)**
BOTTLE   BOTTLE

△ NATURAL SHAPED
The holes must face upwards so the milk sprays over the roof of the mouth.

△ UNIVERSAL TEAT
Flow rates vary, so check at each feed for two to three drops of milk a second.

△ SILICONE TEAT
These last up to a year, whereas latex teats deteriorate after about one month.

△ STANDARD TEAT
Teats for young babies are shorter. Throw away worn or bitten teats.

△ MEASURING JUG   △ PLASTIC FUNNEL   △ SCISSORS FOR CARTONS   △ SPOON & KNIFE   △ SALT FOR CLEANING

37

47 WASHING & STERILIZING EQUIPMENT

Milk is the perfect breeding ground for bacteria, which could make your baby very ill, so you need to sterilize all bottles, teats, and caps by one of the methods shown here. But before sterilizing, all items must be washed out thoroughly using a bottle brush with warm water, liquid detergent, and then rinsed well. If you rub the inside of a teat with salt, the scraping action will remove any trapped milk traces from the teat. Then allow all rinsed items to drain on kitchen paper, not the draining board. Don't warm the feed until you need it, or try to keep milk warm in a thermos. After a feed, discard any milk left in the bottle.

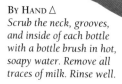

BY HAND △
Scrub the neck, grooves, and inside of each bottle with a bottle brush in hot, soapy water. Remove all traces of milk. Rinse well.

STEAM STERILIZER △
Moist heat destroys harmful bacteria and cleans bottles in less than 10 minutes. The bottles do not need rinsing.

DISHWASHING BOTTLE-FEEDING EQUIPMENT △
This is an easy way to wash your equipment, but it is not a substitute for sterilizing. Set the dishwater on the hot cycle. After the wash use a pin to clear the holes in the teats.

BOIL TO STERILIZE △
Wash the equipment, then boil for 25 minutes with everything fully submerged.

48 MANAGING A BOTTLE-FEEDING ROUTINE

Bottle feed your baby when he seems hungry, not by the clock. Newborn babies often need as many as seven to eight feeds a day, taking about 50 ml (2 fl oz) at each feed. So put at least this amount of feed into each of the six bottles to begin with. By six months you will be making up feeds of 200 ml (7 fl oz). As a rough guide, your baby will require about 150 ml of milk per kilogram of body weight (or 2 ½ fl oz per 1 lb) every 24 hours. Before you begin, check the flow from the teat (there should be several drops per second), and the heat of the milk (which ideally should be at room temperature).

Try a few drops on your wrist first to make sure it is not too hot. After six months on infant formula, your baby may need supplements of iron or vitamin D, or may need to be put on follow-on milk which has extra protein and vitamins (*see chart below*). If in doubt, check with your surgery.

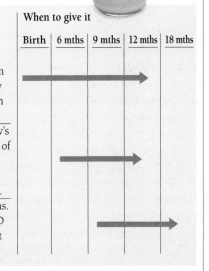

MEASURING JUG ▷
If you do not want to mix the formula directly in the bottle, or if you use disposable liners, you will need a measuring jug.

Type of milk	What it is	When to give it				
		Birth	6 mths	9 mths	12 mths	18 mths
Infant formula	This is cow's milk modified to resemble human breast milk. From 6 months your baby may need supplements of iron and vitamin D.					
Follow-on formula	This is also modified cow's milk intended for babies of 6 months or over. It has iron and vitamin D, so supplements not needed.					
Whole cow's milk	Begin this from 9 months. Extra iron and vitamin D may still be needed. Part of a pre-school diet.					

49 MAKING UP A POWDER FORMULA

Infant powder formula usually comes as a powder in tins, which you mix up as needed. You will need to have a supply of made-up bottles in the fridge ready to give as soon as they are needed. Make up the correct levels following the instructions on the tin exactly. You can do one bottle, or a batch of bottles, at a time, whichever is more convenient for you. With the measuring scoop from the formula pack, add loosely filled scoops to each measure of water as directed. Always start with fresh cold water from the mains, boiled, and cooled once. Never use mineral water. You can mix the formula directly into the bottle(s), or via a jug. Once poured, seal the bottle with the disk and ring, but not the teat, and shake well to mix.

2 △ Open the tin. Use the scoop inside to take the powder. Level off with the back of a knife.

Hold the bottle at eye level to check you have the correct fluid level required

1 △ Rinse your equipment with boiled water, drain, and clean your hands. Fill the kettle with fresh water and boil. Pour the boiled water into the bottles, filling them to the correct level for your measure.

3 △ Don't pack the powder. Drop each scoop into the bottle. The powder quickly dissolves.

50 STORING MILK CORRECTLY

Once the formula is mixed and shaken, take the disc and ring off the bottle. Put the teat in upside down, but don't let it dip in the milk – empty some out if necessary. Reseal the disc and ring. Fill all the bottles and put the caps on. Store them in the fridge, ideally on a tray so they don't fall over, and not inside the door. Do not store for longer than 24 hours.

Don't let the upside-down teat touch the milk

51 GETTING THE BOTTLE READY

For each feed, take the bottle from the fridge and turn the teat the right way up. Warm the bottle in warm water, or at least bring it up to room temperature. Never warm the bottle in a microwave oven because the milk may become dangerously hot.

1 △ Place the bottle right side up in a bowl of warm water, or under a hot tap, shaking it all the time.

2 △ Check the flow of milk: you should be getting two or three drops per second. If you are not, change the teat.

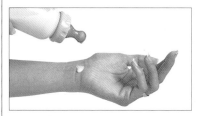

3 △ Test the milk temperature tipping a few drops on your wrist. It should feel tepid, although cold milk is safe.

4 △ To keep the flow going, screw the ring so it just stays on the bottle. This allows air in as your baby sucks milk out.

52 GIVING A BOTTLE FEED

The beauty of bottle feeding is that it allows mother some time off from the relentless feeding duties, and gives father and baby an ideal time to cuddle and bond together. Whoever is giving the bottle feed – parent, childminder, or grandparent – needs to hold her close and talk and smile at her. Put a bib on her. Lie her half-sitting, cradled in the crook of one arm, your hand supporting her buttocks and legs. Stroke her near cheek which should start the sucking reflex. Give her the teat.

HOLD BABY SEMI-UPRIGHT

53 WHEN BABY WON'T LET GO

When your baby has finished drinking the milk, pull the bottle firmly away. If she still wants to suck, offer her your clean little finger. However, if she doesn't want to let go of the bottle, slide your little finger between her gums and alongside the teat. This will break the suction of the teat.

PUT LITTLE FINGER IN CORNER OF MOUTH

54 SLEEPING DURING A FEED

If your baby dozes off during a feed, she may have wind which is making her feel full. Sit her more upright and burp her (*see opposite*) for a couple of minutes. Then offer her more milk. Remember to tilt the bottle at an angle so that the teat is full of milk, not air. She'll decide when she's had enough.

REMOVE THE TEAT & WAKE HER

55 SWITCHING FROM BREAST TO BOTTLE

Even if you want to bottle-feed, breast-feeding for at least two days will give your baby valuable antibodies to help fight infection. You can then switch from breast to bottle if you decide not to carry on. But if you start by bottle-feeding, you cannot then switch to breast feeds. If you do change over, give baby time to adjust. Replace a lunchtime breast-feed with a bottle every third day. Moisten the teat with a few drops of breast milk to help. After three days, swap a second daytime feed; then three days later a third, then the night feed.

56 BURPING YOUR BABY

Allow your baby the chance to burp up any swallowed air, or "wind". That wind may make her feel full. If she doesn't burp after 30 seconds, don't worry: it's still good for both of you to pause, relax, and slow down at a feed.

Rub her back to encourage a burp

Have a clean fabric nappy on your shoulder

△ BURPING A NEWBORN
Put a very young baby against your shoulder supporting her floppy head under your chin. She may well bring up some milk (known as possetting).

△ FORWARDS LEAN
Sit her leaning slightly forwards on your lap. Jiggle and rub her back.

◁ ACROSS THE LAP
Support your baby on your lap, face-down. Rub her back rhythmically.

FIRST MEALTIMES

57 FIRST UTENSILS & BIBS

For first meals buy an unbreakable baby bowl, spoon, and beaker. Start with weaning spoons that have long handles and small, shallow, rounded recesses so they will not hurt baby's mouth. Buy a bowl with a non-slip bottom to stop baby knocking it off the tray. Some also come with a useful storage lid. Baby food pots and spoons suitable for storing home-prepared food in the fridge or freezer are also handy. A plastic juice box holder helps prevent spills if baby drinks from a carton. Always have two beakers: one for home use, and one that prevents spillage in transit. Buy several towelling bibs with plastic backing, an apron bib, and a plastic bib with tray. You also need a hand-held blender, or liquidizer, and coarse grater to prepare the food.

△ PLASTIC BOWL

△ FIRST SPOON

△ TWO-HANDED & NO-HANDLE PLASTIC SIPPY CUPS

△ PLASTIC BIB

△ FOOD PROCESSOR

△ APRON BIB

△ FABRIC BIB

58 HIGHCHAIR HINTS

Once baby is sitting up you will need a highchair. Make sure it is sturdy and easy to clean. Natural wood or reinforced plastic are fine. Either should have a detachable plastic tray. The tray must be large and have a rim. Check for eyelet holes, or "D" rings, for a separate safety harness, as well as for an integral crutch strap.

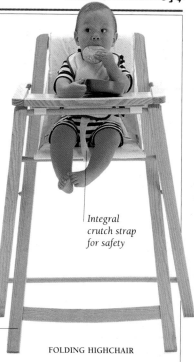

Integral crutch strap for safety

FOLDAWAY ▷
Chairs that fold away compactly are very handy if space is tight.

Padded seat with steel frame support

△ **TABLE SEAT**
Ideal for travelling, this seat can be fixed simply and securely to a table top.

Sturdy pine legs that fold away after use

FOLDING HIGHCHAIR

59 FIRST FOODS FOR 4–6 MONTH-OLDS

Introduce solids when your baby is not too hungry or tired, and you are relaxed. Start with rice mixed with breast- or formula-milk or cooled boiled water, to make it smooth and sloppy and easy to digest. Semi-liquid puréed carrot, apple, or potato, without any lumps, is ideal at this stage. Peel fruit and vegetables carefully, and remove all pips and string. Then steam or boil, and purée or sieve.

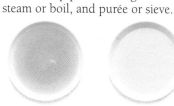

SEMI-LIQUID RICE   **PURÉED CARROT**   **PURÉED APPLE**   **PURÉED POTATO**

60 FIRST FOODS FOR 6–8 MONTH-OLDS

Stick to fresh foods that can be mashed or minced to the texture of cottage cheese. Add liquid or yogurt to help you to achieve this texture. Peel fruit or vegetables carefully, removing any pips and strings. You can also start to give your baby sticks of raw vegetables, such as carrot, to suck on. Trim off fat and skin from fish or meat, and grill or poach where possible. Remove any bones and mince finely.

MINCED CHICKEN   MINCED FISH   MASHED BOILED EGG

△ **FIRST FINGER FOODS**
Shapes made from cheese or banana, and some bread, are ideal to suck and eat.

61 FIRST FOODS FOR 8–9 MONTH-OLDS

You can now introduce chunkier textures, so try chopping food rather than mashing. Cook and prepare food as for a younger baby. Include foods such as toast, home-made lasagne, shepherd's pie (without salt), and soups. Keep giving plenty of finger foods.

△ MASHED LENTILS

△ RICE

△ **MORE FINGER FOODS**
Cut sticks and shapes from carrots and celery as well as slices from apple, avocado, peach, and apricot to offer your baby different textures and flavours. These are also ideal for sucking.

△ PASTA

△ LEAN MINCE

62 FOODS FOR 10–12 MONTH-OLDS

At this stage your baby can progress to what the rest of the family is eating, but chopped up into bite-sized pieces. Keep salt out of the diet (add table salt to your own plate if needed). Introduce stews, well-cooked pork, and steamed broccoli and cabbage as part of the diet. Tinned tuna drained and flaked into pieces is also suitable. You can also try out fruits such as orange and raspberry.

BROCCOLI

CHOPPED CHICKEN

GREEN BEANS

TINNED TUNA

NEW FRUITS

63 FOODS TO AVOID

Do not give whole egg before eight months (but egg yolk is fine from six months). Make sure eggs are fresh and cook well. Spinach, turnip, and beetroot should not be given to babies under six months. Avoid salty, fatty, and sugary foods. Use sugar sparingly. Semi-skimmed milk is not suitable for children under two, and skimmed milk is unsuitable before five years of age. Do not give peanuts to a baby.

AVOID NUTS: BABIES CAN CHOKE ON THEM

64 SPOONFEEDING

To get a baby used to the *idea* of spoonfeeding, give her a teaspoon or plastic weaning spoon of baby food between two halves of her normal milk feed. Hold her on your lap, and put the tip of the spoon gently between her lips so she can suck the food. Do not push it in. Be prepared for a mess while she gets used to spoonfeeding.

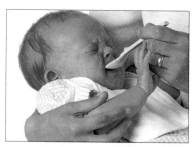
COAT THE TIP OF THE SPOON WITH FOOD

OUT & ABOUT WITH YOUR BABY

70 CHOOSING THE RIGHT OUTDOOR CLOTHING

Babies lose heat rapidly, so in cold weather dress your baby in a padded, water- and windproof all-in-one outdoor suit. To prevent warmth escaping from his head, hands, and feet, put on mittens, bootees, and a hat. Underneath he should still be wearing a stretchsuit, vest, socks, and a knitted cardigan, or jumper.

△ FABRIC
BOOTEES

△ COTTON/ACRYLIC
JUMPER

△ TIE-ON
MITTENS

△ WARM HAT

△ KNITTED SCARF

▽ WET
WEATHER
BOOTS

△ WEATHERPROOF SUIT

71 COPING WITH CHILLING

Look out for tell-tale signs that your baby is too cold: crying and restless behaviour, along with having cold hands and feet are the first signs of body heat loss. Warm up your baby by feeding him in a heated room. Take his temperature (*see p.64*). If it falls below 35° C (95° F), call the doctor.

72 CHOOSING A PRAM OR PUSHCHAIR

A traditional pram is best for a young baby as it protects from draughts and fumes, and allows your baby to lie flat. A carrycot on a chassis is also suitable – some types convert to take a pushchair seat. From three months, a rigid-backed pushchair is fine; however, umbrella-type folding pushchairs are not suitable for babies under six months.

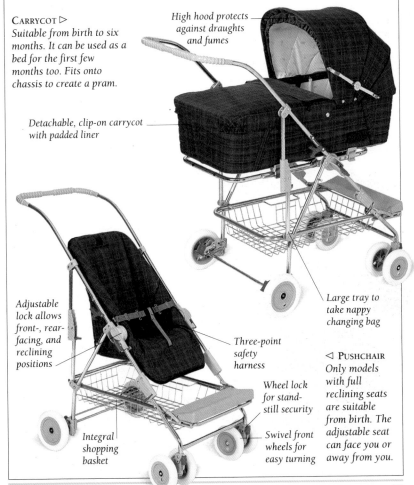

CARRYCOT ▷
Suitable from birth to six months. It can be used as a bed for the first few months too. Fits onto chassis to create a pram.

Detachable, clip-on carrycot with padded liner

High hood protects against draughts and fumes

Large tray to take nappy changing bag

Adjustable lock allows front-, rear-facing, and reclining positions

Three-point safety harness

Wheel lock for stand-still security

Integral shopping basket

Swivel front wheels for easy turning

◁ PUSHCHAIR
Only models with full reclining seats are suitable from birth. The adjustable seat can face you or away from you.

73 CHOOSING A BABY CAR SEAT

You will need two different types of car seat in your baby's first two years, depending on his height and size. For babies up to 10 kg (22 lb), rearward facing seats can be used in the front or rear of your car. They have an integrated harness with crutch strap for protection. For babies from 9–18 kg (20–40 lb) forward facing seats with a five-point harness are suitable. Consider combined types as well.

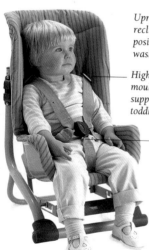

Upright to reclining position, and washable cover

High back with moulded sides to support baby and toddler

Adjustable five-point harness

△ FIRST STAGE SEAT
Rear-facing seats can be secured with a proper lap and shoulder seat belt in a front or back seat. Many come with a built-in handle for easy lifting when baby is asleep. Do not use these seats in passenger seats with air bags.

◁ SECOND STAGE SEAT
These are heavy chairs to reflect the growing weight and size of your baby. They have built-up side wings for extra protection. Secured correctly, they can be used in either the front or back seat.

74 IN-CAR SAFETY ESSENTIALS

Always bear in mind the following safety tips when driving:

- Never allow a baby or a young child to travel unrestrained in your car, however short the journey.
- Insist that your child is properly secured in a car seat or is wearing an appropriate, approved restraint.
- Provide a head support cushion or a first stage seat, which your baby will need for a few months.
- Never buy or use a secondhand car seat as the protective structure may be invisibly damaged.

75 CONTENTS FOR A CHANGING BAG

A fabric-covered changing bag with detachable PVC changing mat, and/or internal PVC lining, is a must for any excursions outside of the home. Make sure the bag has an adjustable shoulder strap and handle for ease of carrying. Check also for elasticated internal pockets to separate nappy-changing items from spare clothes, bibs, and feeding items. Make sure you pack a few spare disposable nappies, nappy sacks for soiled or wet nappies, baby wipes, cotton wool, lotion, a beaker, ready-to-eat solids, weaning spoons, a container of diluted juice, and also a favourite board book and cuddly toy.

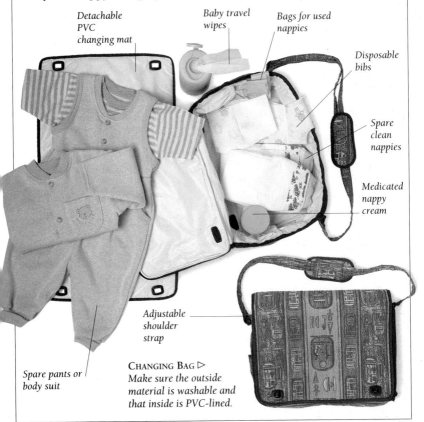

Detachable PVC changing mat

Baby travel wipes

Bags for used nappies

Disposable bibs

Spare clean nappies

Medicated nappy cream

Adjustable shoulder strap

Spare pants or body suit

CHANGING BAG ▷
Make sure the outside material is washable and that inside is PVC-lined.

76 BACKPACKING YOUR BABY

The beauty of a baby backpack is the freedom it gives you to move unhindered with your baby along busy urban streets, or over country fields and pathways. The close contact reassures your baby, he gets a great view, and you are left with your hands free. Backpack carriers are suitable when your baby can hold his head up. Many have a zip-on storage bag, and come with an add-on rain hood.

Padded head and back rest

Lightweight but sturdy frame support

Hip belt and lumbar support

◁ BACKPACK
Look for a padded head support and shoulder straps. A free-standing frame is handy.

Integral and adjustable three-point safety belt

Upholstered and high-backed chair

Support bars securely fixed to bike frame

Foot-guard to stop contact with spokes

77 SAFE CYCLING

Cycling with your baby provides all sorts of short trip opportunities without the bother of a carrycot or car. But your baby's comfort and safety must come first. Harnesses and a helmet are crucial. Seats are ideal from 9 months up to six years (or around 22 kg / 45 lb, depending on the make). Remember your bike will react differently with the extra weight of seat and baby.

BABY ▷
SAFETY
HELMET

SLEEPING & COMFORT

78 CHOOSING COTS

When choosing a cot, make sure it is made of natural wood, is covered with non-toxic paint, has a drop-side mechanism that is secure against baby handling, has bars that are correctly spaced (so baby cannot get his head trapped between them), and has no sharp edges. Many models have two mattress positions: high for newborn babies and low for older, more active babies.

△ MOSES BASKET

Sand down any sharp edges if necessary

Gaps of about 2¹/₂– 6 cm (1–2¹/₂ in)

Baby tamper-proof dropside mechanism

Bars at head should be narrower than along sides

Some dropsides have safety locks

A cot bumper protects against head bumps

FIRST COT ▷

79 COVERING UP

Your baby should be warm in bed but not hot. Buy a room thermometer and maintain an ideal temperature of 18° C (65 °F). At that temperature your baby needs a sheet and three layers of blanket, or sheet and tog quilt. Turn the sheet down over the top edge of the blanket or quilt, and tuck in around mattress edges. If too cold or hot, add or take away a layer to keep a flow of air.

80 LISTENING IN

Baby monitors allow you to relax or do the chores at home while baby is asleep. They plug in to your electricity wall sockets and are designed to pick up baby's sound and other room noises. Look for "listeners" with power-on indicators, pre-set volume safety minimum, and a built-in comfort light.

BABY LISTENER

81 STIMULATING & SOOTHING COT TOYS

Put mobiles and colourful pram toys above and around your baby's cot. Such toys help to stimulate even the youngest baby's interest in the world about him. They encourage shape and colour recognition as well as looking skills. But remember a baby can only focus on things around 20 to 30 cm (8 to 12 in) away. Your baby will be alerted to the shapes, colours, and movement of the hanging objects.

MOBILE TO CATCH THE EYE

82 SOUND STEPS FOR A SOUND SLEEP

The most important thing you can do is ensure that your baby goes to sleep on her back.
- Relax your baby with a gentle bath and some reading time.
- Ensure the room temperature is warm, about 16-20°C (65-68°F).

- Don't smoke in the baby's room.
- Check your baby hasn't got a wet or soiled nappy before bed.
- Before leaving the room check she is breathing regularly.
- Make sure the baby listener is "on" before leaving the room.

83 HOW MUCH WILL MY BABY SLEEP?

At first your baby is likely to sleep in short bursts at any time during the day or night. In the coming months her longest sleep will coincide more with night-time and her wakeful periods will extend in the daytime. From six months, you should start a bedtime ritual, and also keep baby's daytime nap to less than two hours.

Age of baby	Night-time						Daytime															Night	
	1	2	3	4	5	6	7	8	9	10	11	12	1	2	3	4	5	6	7	8	9	10	11
1 month																							
3 months																							
6 months																							
12 months																							
18 months																							

■ Night time sleep ■ Daytime sleep

84 SETTLING YOUR BABY

Dress your baby for bed in a stretch suit or nightdress to allow easy access for nappy changing during the night. In very warm weather a vest and nappy is sufficient. Give him a comfort suck of the breast or bottle if he wants one. Darken the room if necessary to create a soothing environment. An older baby may climb out from under the blankets and lie on top, falling asleep sideways across the cot. He can get his arms stuck in the bars and cry to be freed. To avoid this, try placing him halfway down the cot so that he is less likely to throw off his covers.

SAFE SLEEPING ▷
Medical evidence shows that the safest way for a baby to sleep is on his back. Most countries now follow this practice.

85 SETTLING BABY FOR SLEEP

A breast- or bottle-feed for a younger baby will often be enough to send her to sleep. But there will be many occasions when she needs you to help her relax. At this stage she still needs a quiet time in your arms to help soothe her. After six months you will need to establish a settling-for-sleep routine because she won't be so ready to go to sleep. This "routine" should be a time of fun and intimacy, but with clear signposts that your baby comes to associate with bedtime – bathing, drying, changing into a sleepsuit, play time, and finally putting to bed using soothing contact, gentle rocking, and lullabies.

△ CUDDLES & LULLABIES
Rub her tummy round and round, and sing gently to her until her eyelids close.

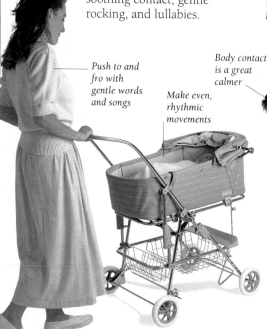

Push to and fro with gentle words and songs

Make even, rhythmic movements

Body contact is a great calmer

△ SOOTHING SUCKING
Up to three months, let her suck your clean little finger, or a natural-shaped dummy, to help soothe her.

◁ RHYTHMIC MOVEMENTS
Keep her in her carrycot and use its smooth, swaying motion to send your baby to sleep.

86 TAKING A BABY INTO BED

When your baby is young and still breast- or bottle-feeding, it is perfectly alright to take her into your bed. Night feeds are easier if you do, and there is no risk of lying on her, provided neither you nor your partner are intoxicated. Of course it can become a habit that is difficult to break, so you must set the rules before the habit sets in deep, and certainly by the time of weaning (*see p.48*).

87 COPING WITH AN EARLY RISER

Early morning waking is actually a sign that your baby has had enough sleep – even if that doesn't help your cause! Leave some toys in her cot overnight for when she wakes, plus perhaps a drink, but in a non-spill beaker, as babies are very often thirsty when they wake. A change of nappy may give you extra rest time. These aids may keep her soothed and prevent her from crying or whimpering for attention.

88 ESTABLISHING A BEDTIME ROUTINE

Sooner rather than later you must establish a going-to-bed pattern that your baby becomes familiar with and accepts. It is up to you and your partner to choose a bedtime that fits in with your own routine – late enough so you are both home, but not so late that baby is beyond soothing and the routine takes up all evening. Any time from 6 to 8 PM is most common. Whatever activities you include in the routine, share them with your partner.

READING A STORY ▷
Story-telling and involving her with boardbooks are great ways of helping you and your baby unwind. This is a time for bonding, and for prompting and responding to her reactions.

89 WAKING FOR A FEED

Even after six months, when your baby no longer needs a night feed, she may develop a pattern of waking for a feed. If she does, make sure firstly she does not fall asleep during her bedtime feed. She needs to learn to fall asleep without relying on sucking. If she wakes, go in at intervals to reassure her, but do not give in to feeding her.

△ AVOID NIGHT FEEDS
Resist the temptation to comfort your baby to sleep with a feed. For a few nights she may cry for a long time, but eventually she will sleep.

90 OVERCOMING NIGHT WAKING

Reassurance is the key word when overcoming baby's sleep problem. If he whimpers, wait a few minutes before going to him. If he cries, pick him up and soothe him. If he calms down to sniffles, put him back in the cot with lots of gentle words. Go back to bed. If he cries again, call from the bed to reassure him. Wait five minutes before going to him. Then just pat and rub his back. Tuck him up again. Carry on this pattern every five minutes for an hour, then ten minutes the next hour, and so on.

◁ SOOTHERS
A soother can help calm and comfort a newborn or older baby when agitated.

91 DIVIDING NIGHT & DAY SLEEP

Make a distinction between how you treat day and night-time sleep to teach your baby there is a time for play, and a time for sleep.

■ Use a carrycot, Moses basket, or pram for daytime sleeps.
■ During daytime naps make sure she is covered but not swaddled or tightly tucked in.
■ Allow her two hours' nap in the day, then wake her. Give her time to adjust to waking before play or food.
■ Save the cot for night-time sleep, making it part of the bedtime routine, so that she comes to associate that place with sleep.
■ At night swaddle her firmly and tuck her in. Keep lighting dim.
■ At night when she wakes, pick her up, feed and change her nappy if needed, making very little fuss.

92 WHY BABIES CRY & HOW TO SOOTHE THEM

Crying is the only way babies have of telling you they are hungry or thirsty, or of getting your attention. They don't cry for the sake of it. They also cry when they are tired, and sometimes when they wake up. You will learn to recognize certain types of crying, from out-and-out colic screaming (see p.63) to night-time sniffles. In either case you should always respond quickly but without a lot of fuss. The following hints may help:

- Feed him, especially a newborn who will cry even if he has been fed only an hour before.
- Give him a beaker of water.
- Comfort him closely in your arms.
- Give him something to suck, such as a finger or soother.
- Rock him rhythmically and horizontally in your arms.
- Sing and talk to him.
- Change his nappy.
- Hold him upright over your shoulder and rub his back. He may be suffering from wind.
- Lay your baby on his stomach across your lap.
- Walk around the room holding him upright in your arms. Some babies respond well to this motion.
- Wrap a small baby in a shawl or blanket to make him feel secure.
- Distract him with a mobile, hand puppet, or any bright object.
- Let him sit with you for a while while he calms down.
- Carry him in a sling: he will be reassured by your closeness.

◁ OTHER CAUSES OF CRYING
Babies also cry if their surroundings are too hot or cold, or in reaction to your moods, or too much fussing.

93 HOW TO COMFORT & REASSURE A NEWBORN

Very young babies are vulnerable to sudden loud noises, bangs, disturbances, and bright lights and will wake as a result. But newborns will always respond to feeling safe and secure wrapped in a shawl or cuddled in a warm embrace. They also have a strong desire for sleep which is to your advantage. The best ways to soothe your newborn are shown below. Remember gentle motion and gentle sounds are your best resources: rocking, swaying, walking, and dancing while holding the baby in your arms provide this perfectly. So does the motion of a vehicle – but this should be a last resort!

Use a rattle toy to keep his attention

△ PAT HIM
Pat and rub his tummy (and back if needed) rhythmically to calm him down and help bring up wind.

Hold him under his bottom

△ HUG HIM
Hold your baby upright against your shoulder. He will feel secure and will be comforted by the familiar beat of your heart. Always support his head with your hand.

Share feeding with a bottle

△ BOTTLE FEED
The best way to soothe him in the first months is to feed him. With bottle feeding, your partner can share the duties and give you a break.

ROCK STEADY ▷
Sing her lullabies while rocking her on her back in this position. Jig up and down by shifting from foot to foot, and vary the pace of the rocking.

△ BREAST FEED
The most likely reason for crying is hunger. Frequent breast feeds day and night will give him food, suckling, and comfort all together.

Make eye contact to let him know you're there

Firm support from your arms and hands

A picture book can catch his eye

△ DISTRACT YOUR BABY
Your baby may forget why he is crying for a while if you distract his attention with a bright or noisy toy. You can also pick him up and point out things to him in the room to help soothe him.

94 COPING WITH A COLICKY BABY

A baby who cries inconsolably for a few hours a day, usually in the early evening, may have colic. It commonly develops by three weeks and disappears by about three months. It's not harmful but it is distressing. All you can do is give comfort by holding, rocking, or rubbing his tummy. Sucking can soothe for a while, and a dummy may help.

BABY HEALTH & SAFETY

95 READING YOUR BABY'S TEMPERATURE

Tuck the bulb of a mercury thermometer into your baby's armpit for a few minutes. A normal temperature is between 96.8°–99.5°F (36°–37.5°C). If it rises over 100°F (38°C) this may be a sign of illness. If it is still raised after resting for 30 minutes check for symptoms: Is she shivering? Does she feel hot? Check her forehead with your cheek, not your hand, to feel how hot she is. Call your doctor if she is under 12 months, and has a temperature staying over 101°F (38.3°C); or has a fever for over 24 hours.

△ **MERCURY THERMOMETER**

Mercury warms and expands up tube

△ **DIGITAL THERMOMETER**

Hold for about 15 seconds

Highest glowing panel shows your baby's temperature

Dual Centigrade and Fahrenheit scale

Temperature panel reading glows

°F	95	96.8	98.6	100.4	102.2	104
°C	35	36	37	38	39	40

△ **FOREHEAD THERMOMETER**

SIMPLE TEMPERATURE SCANNING ▷
The strip thermometer helps you monitor sudden rises in temperature, but it is not as accurate as a standard thermometer. Press it flat on your baby's forehead.

96 GIVING MEDICINE

Put a bib on your baby because medicines are often sticky, your baby is likely to wriggle, and spillage will occur. Have some nappy wipes or a wet flannel close at hand to wipe clean. Always follow the instructions to the letter, and use a 5ml medicine spoon or sterilized teaspoon. If you use a dropper, measure the dose in a 5ml spoon and then suck it up with the dropper. Squeeze the dose into his mouth. With a baby tube, tilt it slightly, straight into his mouth. If these methods fail, let him suck the medicine off your fingertip.

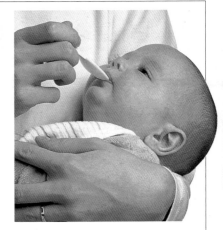

△ SPOONFEEDING MEDICINE
Cradle a young baby as if breast- or bottle-feeding, with his head tilted back.

97 GETTING RID OF CRADLE CAP

Cradle cap is a common type of rash that appears as brown, crusty patches on a baby's head. Rub the scales with baby oil to soften them. Leave the oil on for 12 to 24 hours, then comb his hair gently to loosen the scales. Finally wash his hair – most of the scales should wash away. If it spreads to the baby's face, body, or nappy area, producing a red, scaly rash, buy some emulsifying ointment to keep the areas clean. Do not use soap, baby lotion, or baby bath.

Rub oil onto the affected area

IF SYMPTOMS PERSIST ▷
Consult a doctor if the rash oozes, or does not clear up in five days.

98 GETTING RID OF STICKY EYE

This is a very common, mild eye infection, where the eyelashes gum together after sleep or pus gets in the corner of the eye. Clean your baby's eyes twice a day with cotton wool dipped in warm water that has been boiled. Call the doctor if it does not clear up in three days.

△ COTTON WOOL CLEAN
Wipe each eye outwards from the inner corner with fresh damp cotton wool.

99 SEEKING HELP

It is not always easy to tell if a young baby is very ill, so trust your instincts. If you are at all worried, call your doctor at once if your baby:
- Cries more than usual, or his crying sounds different from usual for over an hour.
- Seems drowsy, listless, unusually quiet, or restless.
- Refuses two feeds, or does not demand a feed in six hours.

100 SAFETY AT HOME

You can minimize the risk of accidents in the home if you take simple safety precautions.
- Place bouncy cradles, Moses baskets, and carrycots on the floor, away from open doors, fires, or table tops. Remove all sharp objects.
- Place special covers over unused electrical wall sockets.
- Keep tablelamp, telephone, and hi-fi cords out of reach.
- Use place mats rather than a tablecloth which baby could pull.
- Install stairgates at the top and bottom of stairs, and a gate across the kitchen door, if baby can crawl.
- Keep a first aid kit on hand.

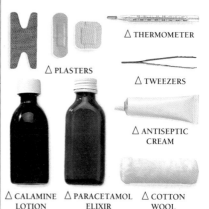

△ THERMOMETER
△ PLASTERS
△ TWEEZERS
△ ANTISEPTIC CREAM
△ CALAMINE LOTION △ PARACETAMOL ELIXIR △ COTTON WOOL

△ FIRST AID KIT
Keep a kit handy with bandages, dressings, adhesive plasters, antiseptic cream, and ointment for cuts and grazes. Scissors and tweezers are good for extracting splinters.

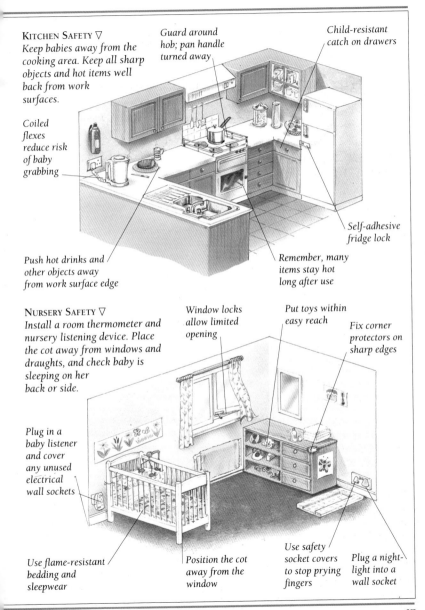

KITCHEN SAFETY ▽
Keep babies away from the cooking area. Keep all sharp objects and hot items well back from work surfaces.

Guard around hob; pan handle turned away

Child-resistant catch on drawers

Coiled flexes reduce risk of baby grabbing

Self-adhesive fridge lock

Push hot drinks and other objects away from work surface edge

Remember, many items stay hot long after use

NURSERY SAFETY ▽
Install a room thermometer and nursery listening device. Place the cot away from windows and draughts, and check baby is sleeping on her back or side.

Window locks allow limited opening

Put toys within easy reach

Fix corner protectors on sharp edges

Plug in a baby listener and cover any unused electrical wall sockets

Use flame-resistant bedding and sleepwear

Position the cot away from the window

Use safety socket covers to stop prying fingers

Plug a night-light into a wall socket

67

101 LEARNING & DEVELOPMENT

Your baby needs your stimulation and responsiveness to develop and learn. He gets that through play, so do not separate play from the rest of the daily routine. Everything should be a game – from unpacking the shopping, or making the bed, to cooking meals. In the first six months he will be largely stationary but will wave his arms and kick his legs. Respond to his facial expressions with plenty of vocal encouragement and close contact. First toys, like a rattle, can be very stimulating. In the second six months he will sit up with no support, start to crawl, and may even toddle around. He will also put anything in his mouth, so be wary.

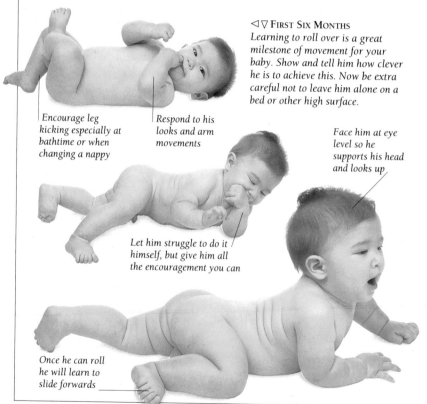

◁ ▽ FIRST SIX MONTHS
Learning to roll over is a great milestone of movement for your baby. Show and tell him how clever he is to achieve this. Now be extra careful not to leave him alone on a bed or other high surface.

Encourage leg kicking especially at bathtime or when changing a nappy

Respond to his looks and arm movements

Face him at eye level so he supports his head and looks up

Let him struggle to do it himself, but give him all the encouragement you can

Once he can roll he will learn to slide forwards

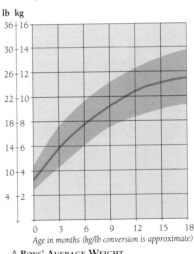

◁ SITTING UP
He will lean slightly forwards with legs splayed out and straight. Put a cushion behind him for support.

△ CLIMBING UP
At around ten months he may be able to pull himself up on to furniture. Check there is nothing unstable in his grasp.

CRAWLING ▷
Getting about and moving on all fours is a great achievement. Some babies go straight to walking without crawling.

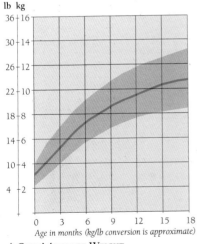

△ GIRLS' AVERAGE WEIGHT
Any weight within the coloured band is normal. A newborn baby may weigh from 2.5–4.5kg (5½–10 lb).

△ BOYS' AVERAGE WEIGHT
Boys, as well as girls, are likely to double their weight in the first six months. Any weight within the band is normal.

69

INDEX

ACKNOWLEDGMENTS

Dorling Kindersley would like to thank Hilary Bird for
compiling the index, Isobel Holland for proof-reading, Fiona Wild
for editorial assistance, Amelia Freeman for design assistance,
Eleanor Rudd for additional modelling, and Mark Bracey
for computer assistance.

Photography
KEY: t *top*; b *bottom*; c *centre*; l *left*; r *right*
All photographs by Susanna Price except for: Dave King 16, 24, 25,
26 (t), 35 (bl), 37, 38 (bl), 39, 40, 41, (tr), 43 (cl), 46, 47 (t, bl),
48 (br), 49, 59 (b), 60 (t), 61, 62 (cr); Antonia Deutsch 32 (b), 33,
34 (t), 35 (br); Ray Moller 27, 38 (tr, cr, br), 41 (b), 42 (b);
Jules Selmes 20, 35 (t), 56 (tr), 62 (bl, br); Steve Shott 52, 56 (cl).

Illustrations
Chris Forsey 67